PATRIOTIC SYMBOLS

The American Flag

Nancy Harris

Heinemann Library
Chicago, Illinois

Customer Service **888-454-2279**

Visit our Web site at **www.heinemannlibrary.com**

Photo Research by Tracy Cummins and Heather Mauldin
Designed by Kimberly R. Miracle
Maps by Mapping Specialist, Ltd.
Printed and bound in China by Leo Paper Group

10 09
10 9 8 7 6 5 4 3

10 Digit ISBN: 1-4034-9379-0 (hc)   1-4034-9386-3 (pb)

Library of Congress Cataloging-in-Publication Data
Harris, Nancy, 1956-
   The American flag / Nancy Harris.
      p. cm. -- (Patriotic symbols)
   Includes bibliographical references and index.
   ISBN-13: 978-1-4034-9379-8 (hc)
   ISBN-13: 978-1-4034-9386-6 (pb)
   1. Flags--United States--Juvenile literature. I. Title.
   CR113.H318 2007
   929.9'20973--dc22
                        2006039381

Acknowledgements
The author and publisher are grateful to the following for permission to reproduce copyright material: ©AP Photo **p. 23** (Koji Sasahara); ©Corbis **pp. 4** (Royalty Free), **8** (Reuters), **10** (zefa/Herbert Spichtinger), **11** (zefa/Chris Collins), **16** (E.P. & L. Restein); ©Getty Images **pp. 5** (quarter, Don Farrall), **19** (Jim Barber), **20** (Royalty Free), **21** (Ron Sherman); ©The Granger Collection **pp. 13, 15**; ©istockphoto **p. 5** (Liberty Bell, drbueller); ©NASA **p. 6**; ©North Wind Picture Archives **p. 23**; ©Reuters **p. 9** (Joshua Roberts); ©Shutterstock pp. **5** (Statue of Liberty, Ilja Mašík), **5** (White House, Uli).

Cover image reproduced with permission of ©Shutterstock (disphotos). Back cover image reproduced with permission of ©NASA.

Contents

What Is a Symbol?

The American flag is a symbol.
A symbol is a type of sign.

A symbol shows you something.

The American Flag

The American flag is a special symbol.

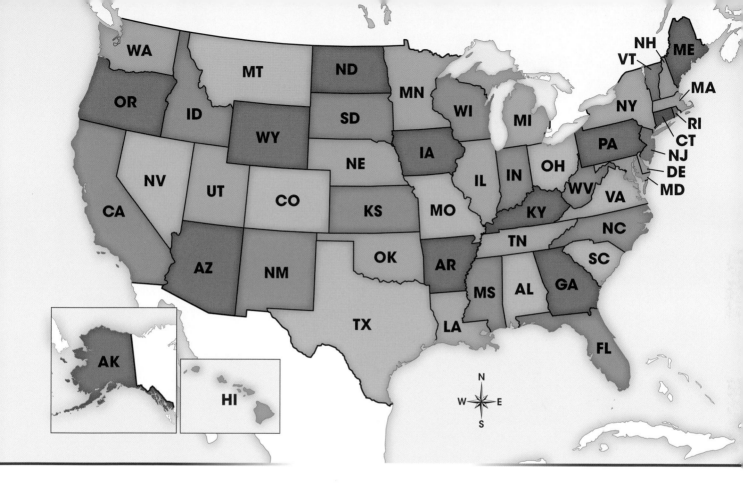

It is a symbol of the United States of America.
The United States of America is a country.

The American flag is a patriotic symbol.

It shows the beliefs of the United States.
The United States is a free country.

Stripes

The American flag has 13 stripes.

It has seven red stripes.
It has six white stripes.

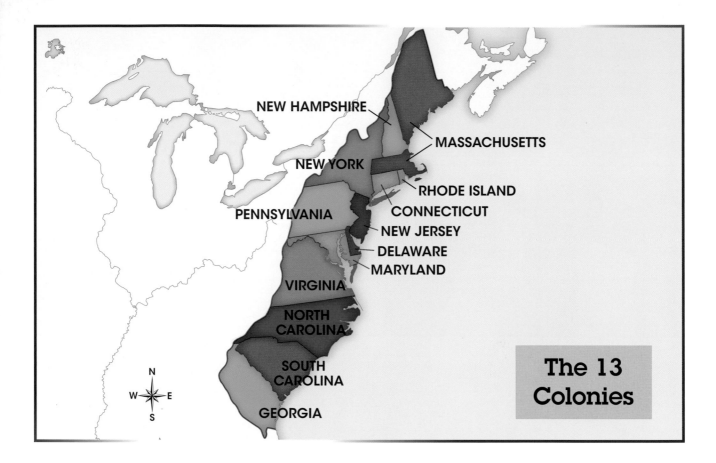

The 13 Colonies

- NEW HAMPSHIRE
- MASSACHUSETTS
- NEW YORK
- RHODE ISLAND
- CONNECTICUT
- PENNSYLVANIA
- NEW JERSEY
- DELAWARE
- MARYLAND
- VIRGINIA
- NORTH CAROLINA
- SOUTH CAROLINA
- GEORGIA

The stripes are a symbol of the 13 colonies.
The colonies were in North America.

A colony is a place ruled by another country.

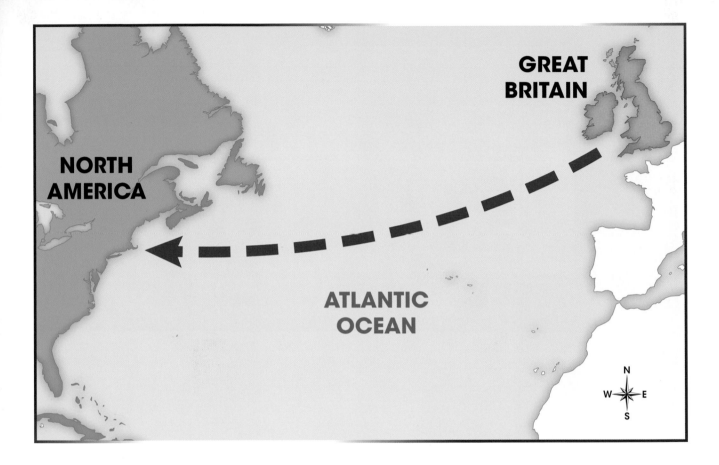

People moved to the colonies to find a better life.

They wanted to be free.
They made a new country.

The new country was called the United States of America.

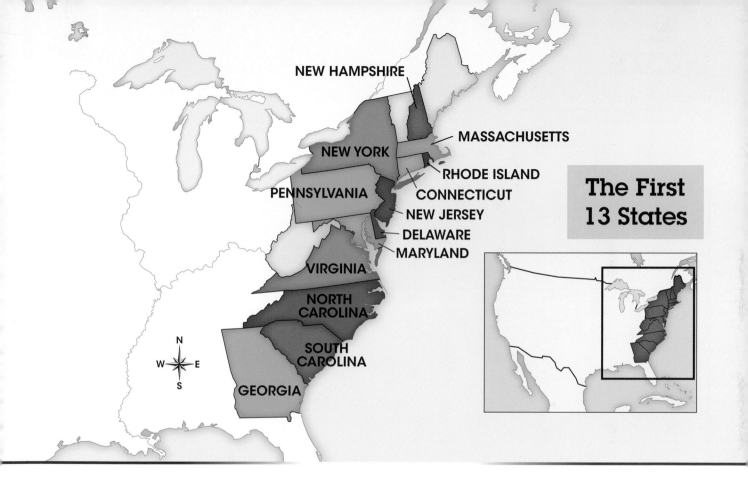

The First
13 States

The colonies were then called states.
At first there were only 13 states.

Stars

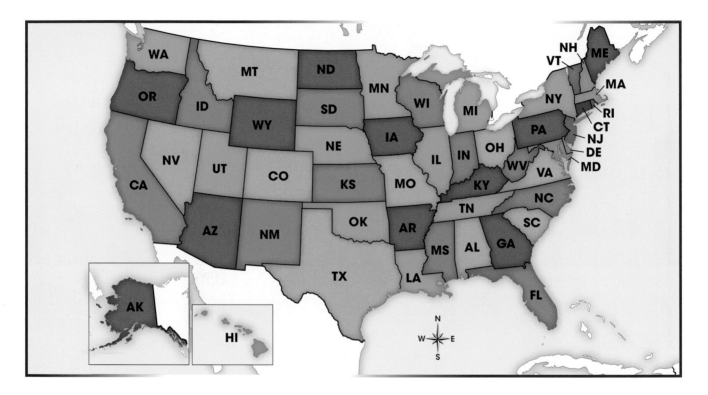

Today there are 50 states.

The flag has 50 white stars.
The stars are symbols of the 50 states.

What It Tells You

The flag tells you that the 13 colonies became free. People fought to make a free country.

The flag tells you there are now 50 states.
People work together to make a strong,
free country.

American Flag Facts

★ The flag is also called "the Stars and Stripes."

★ The flag is also called "Old Glory."

Timeline

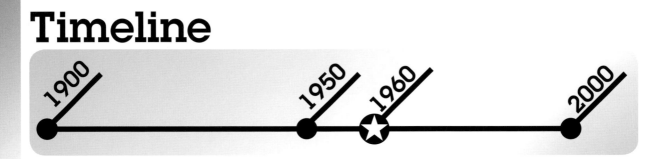

✪ The current flag was made in 1960.

Picture Glossary

 **colony** a place people move to from another country

 **country** an area of land that is ruled by the same leader

 **patriotic** believing in your country

 **state** an area of land that is part of a country. States have their own leaders. They also follow the rules of their country.

Index

Note to Parents and Teachers

The study of patriotic symbols introduces young readers to our country's government and history. Books in this series begin by defining a symbol before focusing on the history and significance of a specific patriotic symbol. Use the timeline and facts section on page 22 to introduce readers to these non-fiction features.

The text has been carefully chosen with the advice of a literacy expert to enable beginning readers success while reading independently or with moderate support. An expert in the field of early childhood social studies curriculum was consulted to provide interesting and appropriate content.

You can support children's nonfiction literacy skills by helping students use the table of contents, headings, picture glossary, and index.